Be a History Detective

Tudor War

Katie Dicker

WAYLAND

This book is a differentiated text version of
The History Detective Investigates Tudor War
by Peter Hepplewhite

This edition first published in 2009 by Wayland

Copyright © Wayland 2009

Wayland
Hachette Children's Books
338 Euston Road
London NW1 3BH

Wayland Australia
Level 17/207 Kent Street
Sydney NSW 2000

Editor: Victoria Brooker
Designer: Simon Borrough

British Library Cataloguing in Publication Data:
  Dicker Katie
  Tudor war. - Differentiated ed. - (Be a history
  detective)
  1. Military art and science - England - History -
  16th century - Juvenile literature
  2. Great Britain - History - Military -1485-1603 -
  Juvenile literature
  I. Title II. Hepplewhite, Peter
  355' .00942'09031

ISBN: 978 0 7502 5702 2

Printed and bound in China

Wayland is a division of Hachette Children's Books,
an Hachette UK Company.

www.hachettelivre.co.uk

Picture acknowledgements:
The publishers would like to thank the following for permission to reproduce their pictures: The Art Archive Limited 26 (top); The Board of Trustees of the Armouries 1 and 6, 7 (top), 10 (left); The Bridgeman Art Library 4 (right), 8 (bottom), 16 (bottom), 24 (top and bottom), 28, 29 (top); Martin Chillmaid 8 (top); English Heritage Photo Library 18, 19 (top and bottom); Fotomas Index 14, 17; Hodder Wayland Picture Library 26 (bottom); The Hulton Deutsch Collection 9; Mary Evans Picture Library 4 (left), 5, 10 (bottom), 11, 12, 13 (left), 15 (top and bottom), 22 (right), 23, 27 and cover, 29; The Mary Rose Trust 20, 21; National Trust Photographic Library 25 (top) (Andrew Butler); Oxford Scientific Films 22 (left) Larry Crowhurst, 22 (top left) (Colin Milkins); The Public Record Office 7 (bottom); Tullie House Museum, Carlisle 16 (top).

Contents

The Battle of Bosworth 4

Becoming a soldier 6

Life as a Tudor soldier 8

Tudor weapons 10

The Battle of Flodden 12

Wounded soldiers 14

The Border Reivers 16

Tudor forts 18

Tudor sailors 20

Life at sea 22

Sir Francis Drake 24

The Spanish Armada 26

Your project 28

Answers 30

Glossary 30

Further information 31

Index 32

Words in **bold**
can be found
in the glossary.

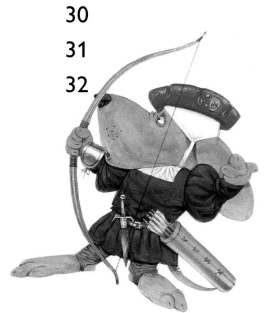

The Battle of Bosworth

The history detective, Sherlock Bones, will help you to find out more about Tudor wars. Wherever you see one of Sherlock's paw-prints you will find a mystery to solve. The answers can be found on pages 30 and 31.

In Tudor times, being an English king or queen was a dangerous job. The first Tudor **monarch**, Henry VII, became king after the Battle of Bosworth. He fought many battles during his **reign**.

The first Tudor monarch

Henry Tudor was a young **rebel** who wanted to become king. In 1485, he marched through Wales with his supporters. King Richard III and his armies caught up with Henry at Bosworth Field in Leicestershire. After two hours of fierce fighting, Richard was dead. England had a new king, Henry VII.

The Wars of the Roses

The Battle of Bosworth is known as the last battle in the Wars of the Roses. Henry VII came from the Lancaster family. His family had a red rose as their **emblem**. Richard III came from the York family – their emblem was a white rose. These two families had been fighting for over 30 years about who should be king.

◀ *Henry grew up in Wales. He was very proud of his country.*

☙ Why did Henry VII have a red dragon on his emblem?

Detective work

Use books or the Internet to find out how many kings and queens had to fight to defend their throne. Draw a timeline of these battles. Start in 1066 with William the Conqueror.

This historian is describing how lucky Henry was to win the Battle of Bosworth:

Richard learned that Henry was some way off, with only a few armed men as his escort... Inflamed with anger he spurred his horse and rode against him... In the first charge Richard killed several men and toppled Henry's standard, along with the standard bearer Willian Brandon. Then behold William Stanley came in with 3,000 men to support Henry. Richard was slain in the thickest of the fighting.

Polydore Vergil, 1510

▼ The Battle of Bosworth was very fierce.

Becoming a soldier

Before Tudor times, armies were made at the request of the king or queen. **Noblemen** were ordered to gather soldiers together. Henry VII knew that some noblemen had become very powerful. He banned them from keeping their own armies in case they turned against him.

Part-time soldiers

The Tudors used part-time soldiers called the **militia**. These men were organised by trusted noblemen. All men between the ages of 16 and 60 had to be ready to defend their local area. They trained for a few days each year. The training was called the summer 'muster'.

▼ *An English army marches through Ireland.*

▶ *This helmet was used in Tudor times.*

Ready for action

Soldiers had to provide their own equipment and weapons. Ordinary workers brought a helmet. The richest noblemen brought horses, armour, helmets, **pikes**, bows and **muskets**. The militia were not allowed to fight abroad. Some men volunteered to fight with the army in Europe because they were looking for adventure, but others were forced to join.

Detective work

Many historic towns had a Tudor militia. Ask your local library if they have a 'muster roll' (like the one shown below).

Captain Barnaby Rich was a soldier during Elizabeth I's reign (1558–1603). He described how some men joined the army:

The constable is loth that any honest man should hazard himself amongst the many dangers of war, wherefor if there hap to be any idle fellow, drunkard, quarreller – or such a one as hath some skill in stealing a goose – these shall be presented to the service of the prince.

✿ Do you think the men described by Barnaby Rich (above) would make good soldiers?

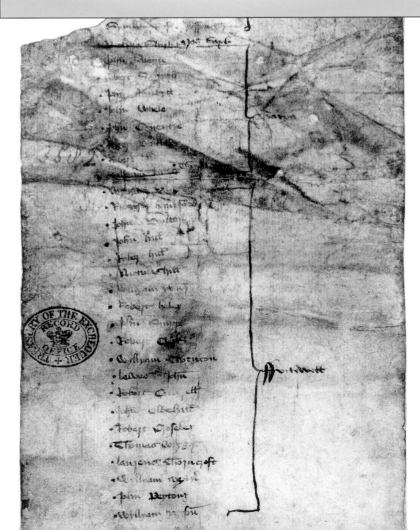

▶ *A Tudor muster roll.*

Life as a Tudor soldier

▶ *There were many different soldiers in Tudor times. Here you can see a musketeer, an archer and a* **bill-man**.

▼ *The illustration below shows a Tudor soldier firing a cannon.*

For most of the 16th century, the best armies in Europe were Spanish or French. However, during the reign of Elizabeth I (1558–1603) there were long wars in the Netherlands and Ireland. English soldiers had to improve their skills to survive these wars.

Recruiting soldiers

In Elizabethan times, over 80,000 soldiers were trained and sent to fight abroad. Some soldiers did not want to fight, but it was difficult to run away – officers watched their soldiers carefully.

The captain

About **100** soldiers fought in a **company**. A captain trained the men and gave them weapons, uniforms, food and wages. The government would pay the captain money to hire his company. Many captains were dishonest – they claimed money for soldiers who had died.

Army conditions

Conditions in the army could be very bad. Men were more likely to die of plague and sickness than of fighting. Because life was difficult, soldiers looked forward to their **ration** of beer. For soldiers fighting in the Netherlands, their ration of beer was four pints a day.

▲ *Soldiers were paid very badly. They often stole money. This cartoon shows a soldier laden with stolen treasures.*

✿ Why do you think soldiers were rewarded with a ration of beer?

This historian is describing a soldier's pay in the army of Queen Elizabeth I:

There are sixteen thousand footmen, distributed into 160 bands, each band having a captain at four shillings a day, a lieutenant at two shillings a day, an ensign at 18 pence a day, two sergeants, a drummer and a surgeon, each at twelve pence a day, and 94 soldiers at eight pence a day.

Fynes Moryson, *Itinerary*, 1598

Tudor weapons

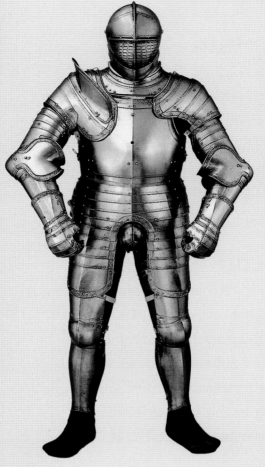

▲ This suit of armour can be seen at the Tower of London.

Tudor soldiers used lots of dangerous weapons. Some weapons, such as daggers, bows and arrows, had been used for hundreds of years. Others, such as handguns, were new inventions.

Tudor armour

Noblemen wore armour. They liked to fight on horseback with a sword and a **lance**. Armour was very expensive. It was passed down from father to son. The best armour came from Germany or Italy. It had curved surfaces so that weapons bounced off the shaped metal more easily. Ordinary soldiers marched into battle on foot. They didn't wear any armour.

Their bows and arrows are thicker than those used by other nations, just as their arms are stronger, for they seem to have hands and arms of iron. As a result their bows have as long a range as our crossbows.

Italian priest, Dominic Mancini, visiting England in 1482–3

▼ Skilled archers carried about 50 arrows. They could fire them all in a few minutes.

Favourite weapons

The most dangerous soldiers were archers. They used **longbows** made from wood. They could shoot an arrow through a wooden door 8cm thick. Other soldiers used spears or **bills**. By the end of the 16th century, soldiers used handguns loaded with gunpowder and larger, heavier muskets. Soldiers who fired muskets were called musketeers.

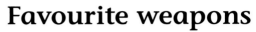

❧ It took years of practice to make a good archer. Why do you think it took so long?

Detective work

Ask your local museum if they have any Tudor weapons. How would a soldier use them? Draw and describe the weapons that you find.

◀ *This musketeer is loading gunpowder into his gun.*

The Battle of Flodden

The Battle of Flodden was fought between England and Scotland in 1513. It was the bloodiest battle in Tudor Britain. James IV, the Scottish king, invaded England with a large army. The English militia challenged James to a battle in Northumberland. James was killed and many Scottish noblemen died with him.

A bloody battle

The Battle of Flodden was fought on a cold, wet afternoon. English cannonballs fired at the Scottish army for over an hour. The Scottish attacked with pikes. But the English had better weapons. Using their shorter bills like axes, they cut the heads off their enemies' pikes.

✿ What weapons can you see in the picture below?

▼ *England and Scotland fought against each other in the Battle of Flodden.*

An English victory

The Scots threw away their useless pikes and took out swords and daggers. Men hacked, slashed and stabbed at each other until they were exhausted. The mud turned red with blood. James IV died like a hero. He killed five Englishmen with his pike before it broke in his hands. The Scots lost 9,000 men while the English lost 4,000.

× battle
✱ rebellion

Tudor battles and rebellions in Britain

①	Flodden, Northumberland	1513
②	Solway Moss, near Carlisle	1542
③	Pinkie, near Musselburgh	1547
④	The Pilgrimage of Grace	1536
⑤	The Western Rebellion	1549
⑥	Kett's Rebellion	1549
⑦	Wyatt's Rebellion	1554
⑧	The Northern Rebellion	1569

▲ A tired soldier returns home after the Battle of Flodden.

Detective work

The site of the Battle of Flodden is now a popular place to visit. Find out if there are any battle sites in your area.

Wounded soldiers

Many soldiers were badly injured in Tudor battles. Pikes, bills and swords made deep wounds. Arrowheads had large spikes that tore the flesh when they were pulled out.

▼ *This illustration from a book by William Clowes shows battle scenes and some of the instruments this surgeon used.*

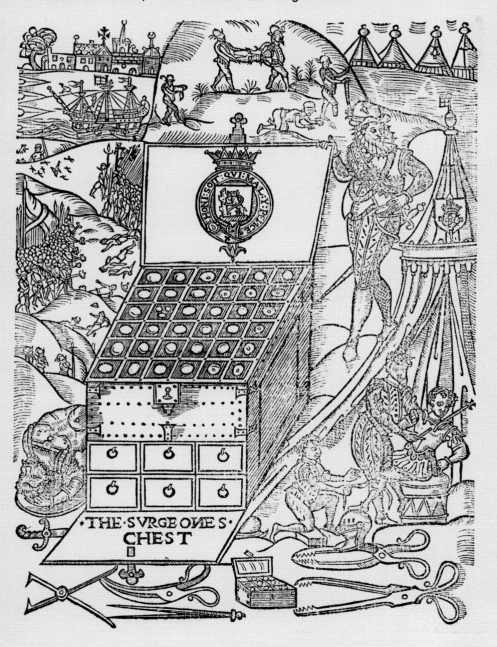

THE·SVRGEONES· CHEST

Treatments

Battlefield surgeons were very skilful but new weapons brought different problems. Gunpowder injuries often meant that an arm or leg had to be **amputated**. Surgeons burned wounds to stop the bleeding and to prevent infection. They did this with boiling oil or red-hot irons.

Surgeons

One of the greatest Tudor surgeons was the Frenchman Ambroise Paré. He used ropes to tie up the ends of **arteries** after a limb had been amputated. Many doctors thought his ideas were wrong, but the English surgeon William Clowes agreed with Paré. He wrote down Paré's ideas for others to read.

♣ Why do you think battles have been called 'the classrooms of surgeons'?

In this extract from 1536, Ambroise Paré talks about new treatments:

When you have cut off the member (limb), let it bleed a little to prevent inflammation.... Verily I confess I used to use various hot irons on the dismembered part. This was a thing of great horror, bringing torment to the patient. I must earnestly beg all Chirurgions (surgeons) to leave this old and too cruel way of healing.

▼ *Ambroise Paré brought new medical treatments to the battlefield.*

The Border Reivers

An area called the Border Marches between England and Scotland was very dangerous in Tudor times. Cattle thieves and murderers controlled the border. They were called the Border Reivers.

A long history

The Border Marches had been a fierce battleground for almost 300 years. For the people who lived there, violence was a way of life. Some families, such as the Armstrongs, Elliotts and Kerrs, could gather small armies together.

▲ *Noblemen tried to keep law and order from Hermitage Castle, in one of the most violent areas of the Border Marches.*

🐾 Look up the word *reiver* in a dictionary. What does it mean?

Detective work

Are you from a family of thieves and villains? Visit this website to find out more about Border Reiver family names:
http://www.reivers.com/namest.htm

Frequent attacks

In 1581, the Elliots from Scotland attacked the area we now know as Cumbria. They stole 274 cattle and 12 horses, robbed nine houses, wounded three men and took one prisoner. This was just a normal attack in Tudor times. The violence continued because the Reivers kept changing their support between England and Scotland. It was difficult to keep law and order.

♣ Look up the word *blackmail*. The Border Reivers gave this word to the English language. What does it mean?

▶ *The Border Reivers rode on horseback and fought with lances and bows.*

A Tudor bishop described the Border Reivers' night raids:

They sally out in the night in troops, through remote by-ways ... The more skilful any captain is to pass through those wild places, crooked turnings and deep precipices, in the thickest mists, his reputation is the greater.

Leslie, Bishop of Ross, 1549

Tudor forts

▲ *This fort in Deal, Kent, was the largest of Henry VIII's coastal forts. It had room for 145 cannons.*

In 1534, Henry VIII made himself head of the **Protestant** Church of England. This brought a risk that the most powerful **Catholic** countries – France and Spain – might attack.

Fort protection

To protect the south coast, Henry built a series of **forts** from Kent to Cornwall. They were different to medieval castles. They had low, thick walls that protected platforms from which guns were fired. Bronze and iron cannons were moved on wheels to fire from any position.

Different forts

During Elizabeth I's reign, a new type of fort became popular. The walls were made of mud and soil. They were covered with stone to absorb the impact of powerful cannonballs. Arrow-headed **bastions** were added to the walls. Their shape offered protection and gave a good view of the surrounding area. They were difficult for enemies to fire at because they were small targets.

▲ *During Elizabeth I's reign, an extra wall was built around Pendennis Castle in Cornwall. Bastions were also added to the walls.*

Detective work

Compare the design of a medieval castle with a Tudor fort. Make your own drawings to show how the design of castles and forts changed.

▼ *This huge Tudor cannon can be seen at Dover Castle. It is nicknamed 'Queen Elizabeth's pocket pistol'.*

❧ Why do you think the cannon was given this nickname?

Tudor sailors

In Tudor times, sailors were very important. They helped to defend England from foreign invaders. The constant threat of attack meant the country had to be prepared. The modern navy began during the reign of Henry VIII.

Detective work

Look at the following website to find out more about the Tudor ship, the *Mary Rose*: www.maryrose.org

▼ *The* Mary Rose *was a great Tudor warship.*

Foreign threats

As an island, England was always under the threat of attack. In Henry VIII's reign, there were more than 50 warships ready for action. New **dockyards** were built on the River Thames and along the south coast. In 1546, an organisation called the 'Navy Board' was set up. This was the start of a full-time navy.

Recruiting sailors

Sometimes, men who worked on fishing boats or trading ships volunteered to join the navy. But in an emergency, the government ordered more men to join. The navy did not pay well and the best sailors often joined pirate ships instead. Their men hoped to make a lot of money by capturing and stealing from other ships.

✿ What stores and equipment do you think were needed on a Tudor warship?

▲ The Mary Rose sank in 1545. In 1982, she was raised from the seabed in a giant cradle.

Life at sea

Life on board a Tudor warship was hard. The crew had to be young and fit. Sailors were paid very low wages. At the end of a war they had no job and no pension. Many sailors became beggars to survive.

▼ Weevils and maggots were often found in sailors' food.

❀ Why did sailors often find maggots in their food?

Food and drink

Sailors had a very bad diet. They ate food that had been preserved for long journeys, such as salted meat, dried fish and dried peas. Instead of bread, sailors ate hard biscuits – softened with beer!

◀ This painting shows a Tudor sailor on board a warship.

In 1599, Vice-Admiral Lord Thomas Howard complained about finding rotten food on board ship:

Both our fish and beef is so corrupt as it will destroy all the men we have if they feed on it but a few days.

▲ *These thieves are being dunked in the sea as a punishment.*

Diseases

Scurvy was an illness caused by a lack of vitamins. It was a common cause of death amongst sailors during the reign of Elizabeth I. Other diseases at sea included typhus, dysentery and plague. Many sailors survived fierce battles but died of disease.

Detective work

Find out about pay and conditions in the Royal Navy today by looking at: www.royalnavy.mod.uk

The Elizabeth Jonas hath had a great infection in her... of the 500 men which she carried... there were dead of them 200 and above. I was driven to set the rest of her men ashore and to make fires in her of wet broom three or four days together and so hoped to have cleansed her of infection.

Lord Howard of Effingham, Commander of the English Fleet, 1588.

Sir Francis Drake

▲ *Sir Francis Drake.*

✿ Drake chose the motto *Sic Parvis Magna*. Use the Internet to find out what this means. Why do you think he chose these words?

One of the most successful Tudor sailors was Sir Francis Drake. He lived during the reign of Elizabeth I. Drake played an important part in the battle against the Armada – a group of Spanish warships.

Spanish attack

Francis Drake was born into a poor family in Devon. He was the eldest of twelve brothers. After serving as a sailor's **apprentice**, Drake joined a group of ships sailing to the West Indies to sell slaves to the Spanish. But the ships were attacked by Spanish ships and most were destroyed. Drake lost a lot of money. He returned home hating the Spanish.

▼ *This map shows the route of Drake's world voyage.*

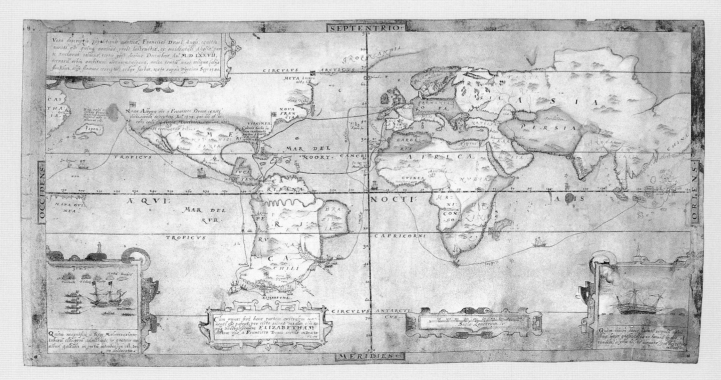

Detective work

Use books or the Internet to find the poem *Drake's Drum* by Sir Henry Newbolt. Where is Drake's Drum today? What are the legends about this drum?

◄ *Drake bought Buckland Abbey with the money from his Spanish treasures.*

World voyage

In 1577–1580, Drake made the first English voyage around the world. When he returned, his ship – the *Golden Hinde* – was full of treasures taken from Spanish ships and lands. Queen Elizabeth I secretly supported Drake's journey. She received £400,000 of Spanish treasure and in return gave Drake a knighthood.

In 1588, Sir Frances Drake played a leading part in the battles against the Armada (see pages 26–27). Drake was a brave leader who earned the respect of his crews. His bold attacks on the Spanish made him a national hero.

The Spanish Armada

In **1588**, the Spanish Catholic king, Philip II, decided to invade Protestant England. He sent a fleet of warships called the Spanish Armada to attack the English navy before invading. But the plans went horribly wrong.

A long battle

The Armada had around 140 ships, but only about 20 were warships. The English had 120 ships, 30 of which were faster and better equipped. They fought at sea for over a week. The Spanish managed to sail into the English Channel. They had over 18,000 men, but they couldn't get close enough to board the English ships and capture them.

▲ *The English ships were very fast. They carried heavy bronze or iron cannon.*

▶ *This map shows how the Armada sailed up the English Channel in a great crescent.*

❀ Why do you think the Spanish ships sailed in a crescent shape?

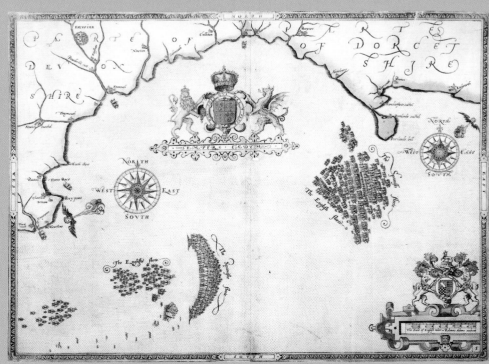

The Battle of Gravelines

On 28 July, the English attacked with **fire-ships** and forced the Spanish ships to separate. In the Battle of Gravelines, the next day, the English navy attacked any ships they found sailing alone. Storms drove the Armada northwards. Many Spanish ships were wrecked as they struggled to sail home. England was saved!

▼ *Tudor sea battles often ended with fierce fighting on board ship.*

Your project

By now you should be fully armed with facts about Tudor wars. This project will help you to find out even more.

Some amazing heroes lived and fought during dangerous Tudor times. Try writing a short life story or a biography about one of these heroes. Choose someone who interests you. Here are a few suggestions:

• The **Earl of Essex** was just 20 years old when the ageing Queen Elizabeth I fell for his charms. But why did war in Ireland cause them to argue?
• **Sir Walter Raleigh** was Elizabeth I's most trusted servant. He was executed in 1618 by King James I. Why was this?
• **Mary, Queen of Scots** was held prisoner by Elizabeth I for many years. Was she really a traitor?
• **James IV** was the young and bold king of Scotland. He helped the French fight against Henry VIII in 1513. Was this wise?

▲ The Earl of Essex.

Plan a project

• Research your Tudor hero or heroine. Use the Internet and your local library. Is there a society, museum or historic site connected to your hero?
• If you were a time-travelling journalist and could interview your hero or heroine, what questions would you ask him or her? Make a list, and then see if you can answer them from your research.

▲ *Mary, Queen of Scots was beheaded for plotting to overthrow Queen Elizabeth I.*

Queen Elizabeth I's most daring sailors were called bold sea-dogs. In 1591, Sir Richard Grenville and the crew of his ship, the *Revenge*, fought against at least 15 Spanish warships. They were brave sailors but after 15 hours' fighting they surrendered. Sir Richard later died of his wounds.

Look out for other brave sea-dogs, such as Sebastian Cabot, Martin Frobisher and Sir John Hawkins – they would make great subjects for your project, too.

◀ *A Tudor ship.*

Glossary

amputate to remove.

apprentice a young person learning a skilled trade.

artery a tube that forms part of the blood circulatory system.

bastion a pointed part on a fort.

bill a weapon that could be used as a spear, hook and axe.

bill-man a soldier who fought with a bill.

Catholic people who believe the Pope in Rome is the head of their religion.

company a group of people who work together.

dockyard an area where ships are loaded, unloaded and repaired.

emblem a type of badge or symbol.

fire-ship a ship that was set on fire before being sailed towards the enemy's boats.

fort a type of castle built for defence.

lance a type of spear used by horsemen.

longbow a type of bow and arrow.

militia a type of army, often formed by local people.

monarch a king or queen.

musket a gun with a long barrel.

nobleman a member of the upper classes.

pike a type of spear on a long wooden pole.

Protestant people who believe that the king or queen is the head of the Church of England.

ration an allowance of food or clothing.

rebel someone who tries to overthrow the monarch.

reign length of time a king or queen rules.

Answers

✤ **page 4:** The red dragon is the symbol of Wales where Henry grew up.

✤ **page 7:** Many of the foot soldiers in Elizabethan times were beggars or thieves. They were unlikely to make good, honest soldiers who could follow orders.

✤ **page 9:** The alcohol in beer was a way of cheering up the soldiers! Some diseases were spread through infected water so drinking beer was also cleaner and safer than drinking water.

✤ **page 11:** Archers were like trained athletes today – the more they practised, the better they became. Archers needed great strength and accuracy to hit their target.

✤ **page 12:** Swords, lances, pikes.

✤ **page 15:** Bad conditions and lack of equipment meant surgeons had only their skills to treat wounded soldiers. They had to learn quickly!

✤ **page 16:** *Reiver:* An old word for robber or bandit.

✤ **page 17:** *Blackmail:* Today it means demanding payment to keep quiet about a secret. To the Reivers it meant demanding protection money – if people didn't pay up they would be attacked.

✤ **page 19:** It was a joke because the cannon was so big. It was a bit like calling Robin Hood's large friend 'Little John'.

✤ **page 21: Weapons** – cannon, handguns, gunpowder, bows and arrows, pikes and bills, swords.
Food – biscuits, beer, salted meat and fish, dried peas, flour.

Sailing equipment – weights to measure water depth, sand glass to measure the time, compass to work out directions, log and reel to measure speed, spare canvas and ropes for the sails, needles and threads, spare pulley blocks for the sails.

Domestic equipment – wooden bowls, spoons, cooking pots, lanterns, clothes, books, games, musical instruments, surgeons' instruments.

❀ **page 22:** Sailors were at sea for a long time so food often went rotten.

❀ **page 24:** It means 'greatness from small beginnings'. Drake was a proud man from a poor background. His motto showed how much he had achieved in life.

❀ **page 26:** The Spanish ships grouped together in a crescent shape to protect themselves. Weaker ships sailed in the centre, protected by stronger warships either side.

Books to read

Facts About Tudors and Stuarts
by Dereen Taylor (Wayland 2007)

Focus on Tudor Life: Tudor Exploration
by Moira Butterfield (Watts, 2006)

Look Inside: A Tudor Warship
by Brian Moses (Wayland, 2007)

Reconstructed: The Tudors
by Liz Gogerly (Wayland, 2006)

Places to visit

Bosworth Battlefield Heritage Centre and Country Park
Sutton Cheney
Nuneaton
Warwickshire
CV13 0AD
http://www.bosworthbattlefield.com

Deal Castle
Deal
Kent CT14 7BA
http://www.english-heritage.org.uk

Look at the Tudor town walls of Berwick-on-Tweed, Northumberland. They were built to defend the town which England and Scotland had fought over for centuries.

Index

Numbers in **bold** refer to pictures.

archer 8, **8**, 10, **10**, 11
armour 7, 10, **10**
army 6, **6,** 7, 8, 9, 12, 16

battles 4, 5, **5**, 12, **12**, 13, 14, **14**, 15, **15**, 16, 23, 27, **27**
  Bosworth 4, 5, **5**
  Flodden 12, **12**, 13
  Gravelines 27
Border Marches 16, **16**
Border Reivers 16, 17, **17**

cannon 8, **8**, 12, 18, 19, **19**
castles and forts 16, **16**, 18, **18**, 19
  Deal Fort 18, **18**
  Dover Castle 19
  Hermitage Castle 16, **16**
  Pendennis Castle 19, **19**
Catholic 18, 26

Drake, Sir Francis 24, **24**, 25

England 6, 8, 12, 13, 16, 17, 20, 21, 25, 26, 27

food and drink 9, 22
France 8, 18

Grenville, Sir Richard 29
guns 10, 11, **11**, 14, 18

Ireland 6, **6**, 8

kings 4, **4**, 5, 6, 12, 13, 18, 20, 21, 26, 28
  Henry VII 4, **4**, 5

Henry VIII 18, 20, 21, 28
James I 28
James IV of Scotland 12, 13, 28
Philip II of Spain 26
Richard III 4, 5
William I 5

musket 7, 8, 11, **11**
musketeer 8, **8**, 11, **11**

navy 20, 21, 23, 26, 27
Netherlands 8, 9
noblemen 6, 10, 12, 16

Protestant 18, 26

queens 4, 5, 6, 7, 8, 9, 19, 23, 24, 25, 28, 29, **29**
  Elizabeth I 7, 8, 9, 19, 23, 24, 25, 28, 29
  Mary, Queen of Scots 28, 29, **29**

Raleigh, Sir Walter 28

sailors 20, 21, 22, **22**, 23, **23**, 24, 29
Scotland 12, 13, 16, 17, 28
ships 20, **20**, 21, **21**, 22, 23, **23**, 24, 25, 26, **26**, 27, 29, **29**
  Golden Hinde 25
  Mary Rose 20, **20**, 21, **21**
  Revenge 29
soldiers 6, 7, 8, **8**, 9, **9**, 10, 11, **11**, 12, 13, 14, 15
Spain 8, 18, 24, 25, 26, 27
Spanish Armada 24, 25, 26, 27

Wales 4
Wars of the Roses 4
weapons 7, 8, **8**, 9, 10, 11, 12, **12**, 13, 14